ॐ

My Beloved Parents (Late) Er. K.P. Bhatnagar & Savita Bhatnagar are a constant inspiration. All my works are dedicated to their Lotus Feet.

ॐ

Contents

FOREWORD

FCS Naveen Bhatnagar

Celebrated Author Globally

OM Sai Ram... Friends, Readers, Dear Students, NBR Today is Your Friend Next-Door.

Blessed to be Mentored by IIM Founders; Govt/Political dispensation and more. Privileged to have Advised Leading Film, Sports Celebrities World-over. From Mahi, Choti Sardarni, Neil John Taylor, Craig Mc Dermott....never ending company, ever-since childhood.

Strong acumen to learning, mentoring helped me make 'SMILE' with a purpose. Equally, blessed over 1,000 Lovely Students in Multi-faceted areas such as Law, Economics, Costing, Accountancy, Financial Management. My Authored Book's (presently 17 Book's, increasing @ 15 Days) seeks your overwhelming support, blessing. **In 07 Hrs Master any Subject.**

PREFACE

NBR Today® provides Bare Act/s, Subject/s of interest for Professionals; Students pursuing Competitive Exams, Professional Courses in form of Ready Reckoner/ Digest/ Guide. NBR Today® is focussed to enhance, support common man's Knowledge, Understanding & gained reasonable recognition amongst Students, Academicians, Professional's, Government. It is easy to read, understand & grasp & for those matters connected therewith or incidental thereto.

Please note with caution that no work is complete, unless supplemented with practice, books, notes, guidance from Teachers, Elders & above all – Parents Love & Respect.

All possible precaution & care has been taken in this material to avoid mistakes & omissions etc. for which the Author/Editor, publisher and /or the sellers are not in any way responsible. All disputes are subject to Delhi Courts. Maximum liability is limited to return amount paid by concerned purchaser/ reader.

Acknowledgements

Author acknowledges invaluable contribution of his **Wife & Daughter**who took considerable pains in the development & review of the title, manuscript. Also, professional colleagues, relatives who took pains & reworked & updated this material to meet, suit requirement of the Reader's.

We will be failing in our duty if we do not acknowledge the contribution of *Amazon, Flipkart, Notion Press, etc.* who helped in publishing & in bringing out this material, publication.

In end, each one of our students is a precious 'Gem' – generation next, entering the new arena, aspiring to seek higher education, especially as professionals, opening new frontiers, all this to unravel "Excellence" as they move up in the higher echelons as Academician, Corporate Ladder, successful Entrepreneur, Home-makers. For sure, your rich idea's, honest feedback will certainly help improve, enrich to serve in a better way.

PROLOGUE

NBR Today® is focussed to enhance, support common man's Legal Knowledge, Understanding & gained reasonable recognition amongst Students, Academicians, Professional's, Government. A number of Voluminous yet Complex Laws affect every Indian's daily chores, which are avidly considered & addressed/answered in NBR Today®. Untiring Journey towards Excellence in the field of Law is what least I get inspired & NBR Today® is one such effort. I continue to do a lot of work for Professional enrichment & Prime importance.

I

THE DISASTER MANAGEMENT ACT, 2005

2. Definitions:-

(a) "Affected Area" Area/ part of Country's affected by Disaster.

(d) "Disaster" catastrophe, calamity, etc. in any area from natural/ man-made cause, negligence, etc. in substantial loss of life, property, etc. beyond coping capacity.

(e) "Disaster Management" disaster planning, etc. & measures to mitigate; respond in its threat; assess severity; evacuation, rescue, rehabilitation, etc.

(m) "Preparedness" readiness to deal threat/ disaster & effects thereof.

(o) "Reconstruction" construction/ property restoration after disaster.

(s) "SG" SG Deptt with DM administrative control & UT Administrator under Art.239 of Constitution.

(t) "SP" DM for whole of State prepared u/s 23.

CHAPTER II: NATIONAL DISASTER MANAGEMENT AUTHORITY

3. Establish NDMA: CG notify it in OG consists Chairperson, Prime Minister of India, ex-officio & upto 09 members, nominated by him;

designate of them, VC. Office term & conditions of service, as prescribe.

4. NA meetings: when necessary, such time, place as Chairperson think fit who presides, if unable, VC preside.

5. Appoint officers, employees, etc.: CG provides necessary them to carry its function.

6. Powers & Function: responsible for DM policies, plans & guidelines, ensure timely & effective response to disaster. NP approve them; Ministries/ GOI Deptts plans approve as per NP; lay guidelines for St. A for SP; lay guidelines GOI Ministries/Deptts prevent disaster, etc., development plans & projects; coordinate enforcement & implementation of policy & plan; funds for mitigation; support other countries as CG determine; such other measures to prevent/ mitigate, capacity build; lay NIDM guideline, policy. Chairperson in emergency, all NA powers, ex-post facto ratify.

7. AC constitute: NA constitute of experts in DM field, practical experience of National, State or DL to recommend, paid such allowances as CG prescribe with NA consult.

8. NEC Constitute: CG immediately after u/s 3(1) notification constitute of GOI Secretary, Ministry/ Deptt DM administrative control be Chairperson, ex officio; similar officials (in all 14) from agriculture, atomic energy, defence, etc. & Integrated Defence Staff Chief, ex officio. Chairperson invite other CG officer/SG taking part in its meeting, such powers, functions CG prescribe with NA consultation. Procedure follow as CG prescribe.

9. Sub-committees constitute: NEC when necessary, constitute one/ more to discharge its functions. NEC from amongst its members, appoints its Chairperson. Expert associate be paid allowance, CG prescribe.

10. NEC P&F: DM related assistance to SGs & St. A assist NA policy, plans, etc. & CG direction for DM comply. Coordinate & monitor DM; prepare for NA approval NP; National Policy implement; DM guidelines different GOI Ministries/ Deptts & St. A; technical assistance to SGs & St. A under NA guidelines; NP implementation monitor; monitor implementation of NA guidelines to prevent disasters & mitigation; measures taken by different Ministries, etc.; evaluate preparedness at all Govt. levels, training; coordinate response in threat; lay guidelines; men/ material for emergency, rescue & relief; assist & coordinate them; technical assist, general education, other functions NA require.

11. NP: Drawn plan for DM for whole Country by NEC regard to National Policy & SG, NA approved expert bodies, etc. on measures to prevention/ mitigate; their integration; preparedness & capacity building; roles &

responsibilities of different GOI Ministries/ Deptts on these measures. NP reviewed & updated annually. CG appropriate provisions under NP. NP copies give to GOI Ministries/ Deptts & draw own plans.

12. Guidelines for minimum relief standard: NA recommend persons affected, drinking water, medical & sanitation; widows & orphans, etc., ex gratia on life loss, house damage & restore livelihood means; other relief necessary.

13. Relief in loan repayment, etc.: NA may, in disasters of severe magnitude, recommend relief in repayment of loans/ fresh loans on such concessional terms appropriate.

CHAPTER III STATE DM AUTHORITIES

14. State DM Authority: Every SG as soon as after u/s 3(1) notify in OG, establish consist Chief Minister be Chairperson, ex officio; who nominate upto 08, include, VC of SEC be its CEO, ex officio. In UT having Legislative Assembly, except Delhi, Chief Minister be Chairperson & other UT's, Lieutenant Governor/ Administrator be Chairperson. In Delhi, Lieutenant Governor be Chairperson & Chief Minister be VC. Office term & conditions be such as prescribed.

15. SA Meetings: meet if necessary, such time, place Chairperson decide who preside, if not attend, VC preside.

16. SA appoint officers, other employees: SG provide necessary to carry SA functions.

17. Constitute AC by SA: when necessary, consist experts in DM, practical experience. Allowances as SG prescribe.

18. SA P&F: Lay down DM policies & plans. State DM policy lay; approve SP under NA guidelines & DM plans SG Deptts prepared; SG Deptts guidelines to integrate disasters prevent, technical assistance, etc.; SP coordinate implement; funds to mitigate recommend; review development plans; review mitigation preparedness by SG Deptts & issue guidelines. SA Chairperson in emergency, all SA powers exercise, but ex post facto SA ratify.

20. State Executive Committee: SG immediately after u/s 14(1) notify, constitute to assist SA & ensure direction comply. It members are SG Chief Secretary, Chairperson, ex-officio; 04 SG Secretaries such Deptts think fit, ex-officio. His P&F, SG prescribe & as SA delegate. SEC procedure discharge functions as SG prescribe.

21. SEC sub-committee: From its members SEC constitute, appoint Chairperson. Expert allowance SG prescribe.

23. SP: Plan for DM for every State prepare by SEC, NA guidelines after consult local authorities, DA & people's representatives required to be approved by SA. It include areas vulnerability to disasters; prevent & mitigate disasters measures; mitigation measures integrated with development plans, etc.; preparedness measures; roles & responsibilities of each SG Deptt; & for them to respond disaster situation. SP update annually. SG make appropriate provisions to finance under SP. Its copies provide to SG Deptts who draw up their own plans.

24. SEC's P&F in disaster: To assist, protect community affected, etc. control & restrict, vehicular traffic, any person; remove debris, etc.; shelter, food, provide, etc. under NA & SA guidelines; direction to concerned SG Deptt, any DA/ other authority, in local limits to rescue, evacuation, etc.; any SG Deptt/authority, etc. provide resources for emergency, etc.; experts, etc. provide advice, etc.; procure exclusive use amenities required; temporary bridges, etc. construct, demolish unsafe; non-Govt. organisations activities carry equitable & non-discriminatory manner; disseminate information to public; CG /SG may direct steps required/ warrant.

CHAPTER IV: DISTRICT DISASTER MANAGEMENT AUTHORITY

25. DDMA constitute: Every SG, after notification u/s 14(1) issued, by OG notify, establish DDMA in every district in State with such name specify. DA consist Chairperson & not beyond other 07 members, as SG prescribe & consist Collector/ District Magistrate/ Deputy Commissioner be Chairperson, ex officio; LA elected representative, co-Chairperson, ex officio. In Tribal Areas, 6thSchedule to Constitution, Chief Executive Member of district council of autonomous district, be co-Chairperson, ex officio; DA's CEO, ex officio; Superintendent of Police, ex officio; Chief Medical Officer, ex officio; (f) upto 02 other DL officers, SG appoint. Where zila parishad exists, Chairperson thereof co-Chairperson of DA. SG appoint not below Additional Collector/ Additional District Magistrate/ Additional Deputy Commissioner be DA's CEO exercise such powers & functions & such other P&F DA delegate.

26. DA Chairperson power: In addition to presiding meetings, powers as delegate. In emergency, power ex post facto DA ratify. DA/he, order, in

writing, delegate to CEO, subject to limitations, deems fit.

27. Meetings: DA meet required & time & place as Chairperson think fit.

29. Appointment of officers & other employees of DA: SG provide necessary for DA functions.

30. DA's P&F: Measures for DM under NA, SA guidelines prepare for district; coordinate National Policy, State Policy, NP, SP & DP; district vulnerable & measures by Govt. Deptts & LA ['them'] undertaken; prevent, preparedness under NA, SA guidelines followed; direct authorities at DL & LA prevent, mitigate, etc. guidelines; monitor DM plans by *them*; monitor its implementation; review preparedness; community training, etc. with LA, Govt. & non-Govt. organisations support; early warnings; DL response plan & guidelines; coordinate response as per district response plan; coordinate LA guidelines disaster prevent, etc.; construction not in order direct to comply standards; buildings, etc as relief center use; establish stockpiles rescue materials at short notice; inform SA on DM aspects; encourage non-Govt organisations involve; communicate systems in order & DM drills; other functions as SG/ SA assign.

31. District Plan: DM plan for every district in State. DA, after LA consult prepare & regard to NP & SP, to be SA approved. Include vulnerable areas; prevention & mitigation measures by Govt. Deptts at DL & LA level ['them']; capacity-building & preparedness by *them*; response plans in disaster, allocate responsibility to *them*; prompt response to disaster; essential resources procure; communication links; dissemination of information to public; Others SA requires. Reviewed & update annually. DP copies to Govt. Deptts at district level and to SA, which forward to SG. DA review plan implement & instructions to *them* necessary.

32. DL plans implement: every GOI office & SG at DL,LA, subject to DA supervise prepare DM plan for prevention & mitigation measures as per DP, assign to Deptt/ Agency concern; DP laid capacity-building. etc.; response plans in disaster threaten etc.; prepare, implement plan at DL level, include LA, etc.; review plan & DM plan to DA submit.

33. DA requisition: Order require officer/DL/LA prevent/mitigate measures, etc. & are bound.

34. DA Powers & Function: assisting, protecting, etc. community in disaster by directing release & resources use by any Govt. Deptt & district LA; control vehicular traffic in affected area; control person movement; remove debris, rescue operations; shelter, food, healthcare etc.; emergency communication; unclaimed dead bodies disposal; recommend SG Deptt/

authority/ body at DL necessary measures; require experts advise; procure amenities; temporary bridges construct, etc.; non-Govt organisations carry their activities; other steps required.

CHAPTER V: GOVT. MEASURES FOR DISASTER MANAGEMENT

35. CG measures: Co-ordinating GOI Ministries/Deptts, SGs, NA, St. A, Govt. & non-Govt. organisations; integrate measures to prevent; allocation of funds; necessary measures for preparedness; cooperation & assistance to SGs; deploy naval, military & air forces, other forces required; United Nations agencies, etc. coordinate; research, etc. institute for train in DM establish; others deems necessary. Other countries affected assist.

36. GO Ministries/Deptts responsibility: Measures to prevent disasters, under NA guidelines; development plans & projects, measures to prevent as per NA guidelines; respond promptly as per NA guidelines/NEC directions; review enactments to incorporate provisions necessary to prevention, mitigation; allocate funds to prevent, capacity-building; assist NA & SGs to draw mitigation plans, etc.; carry rescue operation; damage assess; rehabilitate; resources to NEC/ SEC to such situation, including emergency communication; transport; evacuation, rescue, etc. temporary bridges, etc.; drinking water, healthcare, etc.; other actions necessary for DM.

37. DM plans of GOI Ministries/ Deptts: disaster prevent, mitigate measures as per NP; development plans NA, NEC guidelines; roles, responsibility in preparedness & capacity-building; effectively responding to disaster; present status of its preparedness; measures required perform responsibility specified herein; review annually plan; forward plan copy to CG, which forward to NA for approval. Financing provision; status report on plans herein to NA when required.

38. SG measures: Subject to this Act, each SG follow NA guidelines & measures expedient for DM include coordination its different Deptts, SA, DA, LA & other non-Govt. organisations; cooperate NA, NEC, SA, SEC, DA; assist GOI Ministries/ Deptts in DM; funds allocate to its Deptts under SP, DPs; integrate measures to prevent disaster, plans & projects; integrate development plan, vulnerability of different parts; DM plans by its Deptts as per NA, SA guidelines; adequate warning systems set up; different Deptts & DA preparedness measures; resources of its Deptts available to NEC, SEC, DA to rescue, relief in disaster; rehabilitate assistance to victims; & other

matters necessary for this Act.

39. SG Deptts responsibility: measures to prevent disasters, etc. under NA, SA guidelines; integrate development plans & projects; allocate funds; respond promptly any threat under SP & NEC, SEC directions; review enactments, etc; assist NEC, SEC, DA to draw mitigation, plans, etc.; assess damage; carrying rehabilitation; provide resources with SA consultation at DL; provide resources to NEC/SEC/DA, emergency affected area communicate; evacuation; temporary bridges; essential provisions, etc.; other actions necessary.

CHAPTER VI: LOCAL AUTHORITY

41. LA function: subject to DA direction, ensure on DM train its officers & employees; resources in disaster situation; all construction projects in jurisdiction confirm its standards prevent disasters & mitigation by NA, SA & DA; relief, rehabilitation, etc. in affected area as per SP, DP, other necessary measures.

CHAPTER VII: NATIONAL INSTITUTEOF DISASTER MANAGEMENT

42. NIDM: CG notify in OG constitute such members, term, vacancy fill, as prescribed also its governing body, their powers, functions under regulations. Until regulations in place, CG makes them & NIDM alter/ rescind. NIDM function in NA laid broad policies & guidelines & be responsible for planning, promotion, training, etc. in DM area, documentation & development. NIDM for functions discharge develop training modules, etc. & organise training programmes; undertake training of faculty members; provide assistance to SGs & State training institutes in policies, strategies, DM framework; educational material; mitigation, preparedness promote; organise study courses, conferences, etc. in & outside country; journals, research, etc. publish; etc. other lawful things incidental & other CG function assign.

CHAPTER VIII NATIONAL DISASTER RESPONSE FORCE

44. National Disaster Response Force ['NDReF']: For specialist response to threatening disaster situation/ disaster constitute in manner & service

conditions, disciplinary provisions, as prescribed.

45. Control, direction, etc.: General superintendence, direction & control be vested & exercised by NA & command & supervision of Force vest CG appointed officer as Director General of NDReF.

CHAPTER IX FINANCE, ACCOUNTS & AUDIT

46. National Disaster Response Fund ['NDRF']: CG notify in OG, NDRF for disaster situation threaten/ disaster & credit CG provide after appropriate by Parliament; grants by any person/ institution for DM. NDRF be available to NEC apply towards emergency response, relief & rehabilitation expense meet in CG guidelines with NA consultation.

47. National Disaster Mitigation Fund ['NDMF']: CG notify in OG, NDMF for projects exclusively to mitigate & CG appropriate by Parliament provide. NDMF be applied by NA.

48. Establishment of SG funds: After SA notify constituting & DA, establish State Disaster Response Fund; District Disaster Response Fund; State Disaster Mitigation Fund; District Disaster Mitigation Fund. SG ensure these funds available to SEC; available to SA; available to DA.

CHAPTER X OFFENCES & PENALTIES

51. Punishment for obstruction, etc.: without reasonable cause obstructs any CG/SG O/E or NA/SA/ DA person authorised discharge functions this Act/ refuses to comply their directions, on conviction upto 01 year Jail/ Fine/Both & if results lives loss/ imminent danger, on conviction upto 02 years Jail.

52. Punishment for false claim: to obtain relief, assistance, repair, etc. consequent to disaster from CG/ SG/ NA/SA/ DA officer, on conviction be upto 02 years Jail & Fine.

53. Punishment for misappropriation of money, materials, etc.: Entrusted with them, in custody/for relief in any threatening disaster situation/ disaster, misappropriates on conviction upto 02 years Jail & Fine.

54. Punish in false warning: False alarm of disaster/its severity, etc. lead to panic, on convicted, jail upto 01 year/ Fine.

55. Offences by Govt. Deptts: Head of Deptt be guilty & liable proceeded & punished unless prove all due diligence to prevent its commission. Where

proved consent/ connivance/ neglect any officer, other than Deptt Head, such officer guilty & proceeded against & punished.

56. Failure of officer in duty/ connivance Act contravene: Whom Duty imposed this Act & ceases/ refuses to perform/ withdraws from duties, unless express written permission of superior/ lawful excuse, extend upto 01 year jail/ fine.

57. Penalty for contravening any order u/s 65: 01 year/ Fine/ Both.

58. Offence by Company: or body corporate, every person in charge & responsible to it for business conduct and company deemed guilty & liable proceeded & punished. No offence, if proves without knowledge/ due diligence to prevent it. If provided, consent/connivance/neglect of Director, manager, secretary or other officer they deemed guilty, proceeded & punished. "Company" means anybody, corporate & include Firm/ other association of individuals; & "Director" includes Firm partner.

59. Previous sanction for prosecution: U/s 55 & 56 offence CG/SG previous sanction/officer authorised by thier order.

60. Offence cognizance: No Court take cognizance except, compliant from NA/SA/CG/SG/DA/authority/authorised officer/ person, at least 30 days' Notice of alleged offence, intention file complaint with these said authorities.

CHAPTER XI MISCELLANEOUS

61. Prohibition against discrimination: Compensation & relief provide to disaster victims, not discriminate on sex, caste, community, descent or religion.

62. Power to issue direction by CG: Notwithstanding other law in force, CG lawful direction to GOI Ministries/ Deptts/NEC/SG/ SA/ SEC/ statutory bodies/its officers or employees, as apply to facilitate/assist in DM & such of them bound comply direction.

63. Powers to be made available for rescue operations: Any officer/ authority of Union/ State, when NEC request, any SEC/ DA/ their authorised person, make available perform any functions to prevent disaster/mitigate/ rescue/ relief.

65. Requisition resources, provisions, etc. in rescue operations: NEC/SEC/ DA/officer authorised any resources needed prompt response; premises

needed; vehicle needed, order not beyond period required. "Resources" includes men & material resources; "Services" includes facilities; "premises" means any land, building or its part, etc.; "Vehicle" means vehicle used/ capable to transport, whether propelled by mechanical power/ otherwise.

66. Payment of compensation: Whenever any Committee, Authority/ Officer u/s 65(1), be paid compensation considering rent payable in locality; compelled to change it, reasonable expenses. Aggrieved so determined apply in 30 days to CG/SG, arbitrator refer, compensation amount be paid as Arbitrator appointed by them determine. Where dispute referred by CG/ SG, to arbitrator appointed by them to determine. "Person interested" is who's actual possession of premises requisitioned u/s 65 immediately before/ where not in actual possession, its owner. Whenever any Committee, Authority/ officer, referred u/s 65(1) any vehicle, owner thereof paid compensation as CG/ SG determine on locality fares/ rate prevailing. Provided owner aggrieved by amount matter to arbitrator, CG/ SG determine. Provided if hire purchase agreement, amount determined compensation apportioned between that person & owner & in default of agreement, arbitrator decide.

67. Directions to Media: NA/SA/DA recommend Govt. direct any authority/ person controlling audio/ audio-visual media, etc. to carry warning/advisories threatening disaster situation/ disaster & comply it.

71. Court jurisdiction barred: Except Supreme Court/High Court, no jurisdiction any suit/ proceedings anything done, instruction, etc. by CG, NA, SG, SA or DA under power conferred this Act.

72. Act has overriding effect: Notwithstanding inconsistent other law in force/ instrument having effect any other Law.

73. Good Faith action: no suit/ prosecution/ proceeding in any Court against CG/ NA/SG/ SA/ DA/ LA/any CG O/E / NA/SG/SA/DA/ LA/ any person working for such Govt./ authority done in good faith under this Act/ rules/regulations.

74. Immunity from legal process: CG, NA, NEC, SG, SA, SEC or DA Officers & Employees be immune from legal process in warning impending disaster disseminated by them / action taken/ direction issued.

☙

ABBREVIATIONS

1. Advisory Committee- AC
2. And - &
3. Central Govt. – CG
4. Chief Executive Officer - CEO
5. Department- Deptt
6. District Disaster Management Authority/ District Authority – DDMA/ DA
7. District Level- DL
8. Disaster Management – DM
9. District Plan- DP
10. Government- Govt.
11. Govt. of India- GOI
12. Govt. of the State- SG
13. Local Authority/ies – LA
14. Officer or Employee- O/E
15. Official Gazette- OG
16. National Disaster Management Authority/National Authority - NDMA/ NA
17. National Executive Committee- NEC
18. National Institute of Disaster Management - NIDM
19. National Plan- NP
20. Powers & Functions- P&F
21. State Authority - SA
22. State Authorities- St. A
23. State Executive Committee – SEC
24. State Govt.- SG
25. State Plan- SP
26. Vice-Chairperson- VC
27. Union Territory- UT

www.ingramcontent.com/pod-product-compliance
Lightning Source LLC
Chambersburg PA
CBHW070025260726
48658CB00003B/1038